SAFELY THROUGH THE STORM

•

120

REFLECTIONS

ON

HOPE

•

Debra Herbeck

SERVANT
BOOKS

PUBLISHED BY ST. ANTHONY MESSENGER PRESS
CINCINNATI, OHIO

Book design by Mark Sullivan
Cover design by Candle Light Studios
Cover photo © Silver-John Photography and Shutterstock Images

LIBRARY OF CONGRESS CATALOGING-IN-PUBLICATION DATA
Herbeck, Debra.
Safely through the storm : 120 reflections on hope / Debra Herbeck.
p. cm.
ISBN 978-0-86716-941-6 (pbk. : alk. paper) 1. Hope—Religious aspects—
Catholic Church—Meditations. 2. Catholic Church—Prayers and devotions. I.
Title.
BX1795.H69H47 2010
234'.25—dc22

2010015084

ISBN 978-0-86716-941-6

Published by Servant Books, an imprint of St. Anthony Messenger Press.
28 W. Liberty St.
Cincinnati, OH 45202
www.AmericanCatholic.org
www.ServantBooks.org

Printed in the United States of America.

Printed on acid-free paper.

11 12 13 14 5 4 3 2

*This book is dedicated to my mom, Carole,
whose life and death taught me the difficult
yet transformative lessons of suffering.*

F o r e w o r d

My hope is in the Lord, the Lord alone.

As often as we pray those words, something is eventually bound to happen that poses the question, do we really believe them? The question comes in small ways, maybe even every day, as we experience frustration, disappointment, and pain. Even success— as many of the writers in this anthology note—can shake the hope we have in God, as we are tempted to shift that hope to the things of this world.

The question also comes in big ways. For me one of the most profound challenges on this score came on a February afternoon in 2009, when I received a rather cryptic call from a hospital emergency room. I arrived at the hospital, and after some delay the mystery was cleared up. My husband, age fifty, had collapsed while working out that morning and had died.

All kinds of hope died that morning too: hope for a long and happy second half of life with Michael; hope for two little boys growing up with the role model and support of the great father that he was; hope that the spiritual growth I had experienced as a result of our friendship and marriage, the sanity he had brought to my life, would continue in the framework of our life together.

The months that followed were terribly difficult, as you can imagine. (You are perhaps reading this book because you don't have to imagine; you know.) But in those long nights, days, and weeks, hope shone through. It wasn't anything unfamiliar or new to me. It was the kind of hope I had learned and tried to practice all my life. But now I was called on to live it in a way I had not expected.

The temptation to lose hope—that is, a trust that all things work together in God for good—rested for me on the assumption (one that I didn't even know I had) that nothing like this would happen, that Michael and I would have many more adventures, many more clarifying arguments, and grow old together until…what?

Well, I wasn't sure, but the plan didn't include the reality of his dying without even a chance to say good-bye at the age of fifty.

As time went on I understood how faulty my assumption had been. On All Souls' Day of that year, I went to Mass and heard the priest preach in his homily, "Jesus prayed that this cup would pass by him but then accepted it. How foolish we are to imagine that this cup, which did not even pass by our Lord, would pass by us."

I realized that I had been assuming just that. And a bit of hope was restored in that humble realization, due to two factors.

First came the deeper acceptance of my and Michael's member-ship in this human family that is limited, that suffers, that dies. The hope I felt was related to a deeper sense of communion with others—as well as, of course, with the Lord. He suffered, and he suffers with me and with all those who suffer. We are joined in that one body. The Lord is with us, and with him we will rise.

Another place hope took root in my life was in my journey toward understanding what it really means to put God first. Many of the writers in this book allude to this truth: While we are touched by God through other human beings as well as God's creation, ultimately they all pass, as do we, and so our ultimate, deep hope for happiness, love, beauty, and truth can't rest in them. Life is a beautiful gift, but it is a gift that points to something greater and more lasting.

My experience over the past year is echoed in the succinct, knowing, and truthful words of the great spiritual writers in this book. We will suffer; it is just a fact. In suffering we are tempted to lose hope and faith in the Lord's love and in his desire for our eternal life with him. But that same suffering can teach us, if we let it, to turn to God and place our hope and trust in him. He loved us into existence for reasons that do not disappear as we suffer but indeed, paradoxically, may become all the more clear the deeper into the mystery we plunge, knowing the Lord accompanies us.

—Amy Welborn
www.amywelborn.com

Amy Welborn is the author of many books, including *The Words We Pray: Discovering the Richness of Traditional Catholic Prayers* (Loyola).

The
Quotes

1 | *Our True Hope*

Man's great, true hope which holds firm in spite of all disappointments can only be God—God who has loved us and who continues to love us "to the end," until all "is accomplished" (cf. Jn 13:1 and 19:30).

—*Pope Benedict XVI*

2 | *Emmanuel*

God, in and through Jesus, has become Emmanuel, God with us. It belongs to the center of our faith that God is a faithful God, a God who did not want us to ever be alone but who wanted to understand—to stand under—all that is human. The Good News of the Gospel, therefore, is not that God came to take our suffering away, but that God wanted to become part of it.

—*Fr. Henri Nouwen*

3 | *Trace His Guiding Hand*

Let us humbly and reverently attempt to trace His guid-
ing hand in the years which we have lived. Let us thank-
fully commemorate the many mercies He has promised
to us in time past, the many sins He has not remembered, the many dangers He has averted, the many
prayers He has answered, the many mistakes He has cor-
rected, the many warnings, the many lessons, the much
light, the abounding comfort which He has from time
to time given. Let us dwell upon times and seasons,
times of trouble, times of joy, times of trial, times of
refreshment. How did He cherish us as children!…
He has not made us for naught; He has brought us thus
far, in order to bring us further, in order to bring us on
to the end. He will never leave us nor forsake us.

—*Bl. Cardinal John Henry Newman*

4 | *Be at Peace Today*

Do not look forward to what may happen tomorrow.
The same Eternal Father who cares for you today
Will take care of you tomorrow
And every day of your life.
He will either shield you from suffering,
Or He will give you unfailing strength to bear it.
Be at peace, then, and put aside all anxious thoughts.

—*St. Francis de Sales*

5 | *You Will Not Be Overcome*

[O]ur good Lord spoke quietly without voice or word of mouth…and said so sweetly, "…You will not be overcome."

…This word, "You will not be overcome," was said very distinctly and firmly to give us confidence and comfort for whatever troubles may come. He did not say, "You will never have a rough passage, you will never be over-strained, you will never feel uncomfortable," but he *did* say, "You will never be overcome." God wants us to pay attention to these words, so as to trust him always with strong confidence, through thick and thin. For he loves us, and delights in us; so he wills that we should love and delight in him in return, and trust him with all our strength. So all will be well.

—*St. Julian of Norwich*

6 | *Obedience*

I said, "Let me walk in the fields."
   He said, "No, walk in the town."
I said, "There are no flowers there."
   He said, "No flowers, but a crown."
I said, "But the skies are black;
   There is nothing but noise and din."
And He wept as He sent me back;
   "There is more," He said; "there is sin."

I said, "But the air is thick,
   And fogs are veiling the sun."
He answered, "Yet souls are sick,
   And souls in the dark undone."

I said, "I shall miss the light,
   And friends will miss me, they say."
He answered, "Choose to-night
   If *I* am to miss you, or they."

I pleaded for time to be given.
   He said, "Is it hard to decide?
It will not seem hard in heaven
   To have followed the steps of your Guide."

I cast one look at the fields,
   Then set my face to the town;
He said, "My child, do you yield?
   Will you leave the flowers for the crown?"

Then into His hand went mine,
    And into my heart came He;
And I walk in a light divine
    The path I had feared to see.

—George MacDonald

7 | *Sweet Tribulations*

[T]he God who once freed the three children from the
fiery furnace is with me always; he has delivered me
from … tribulations and made them sweet, for his
mercy is for ever. In the midst of these torments,…
I am, by the grace of God, full of joy and gladness,
because I am not alone—Christ is with me.… In the
midst of this storm I cast my anchor towards the throne
of God, the anchor that is the lively hope in my heart.

—St. Paul Le-Bao-Tinh

8 | *Time to Believe*

When things fall apart and all seems to be ruined and
when the terrible question "What do you do when
nothing makes sense?" comes right home, the answer is
that it is the time to believe. It is the time for faith.…
One must grab onto God.… One must be able to say,
"I believe that God's goodness is going to bring about
some greater good by this horror. It may not be a great
good for me in this world, but it will be a great good
someplace, somewhere, perhaps for those I love in the
next world."

—Fr. Benedict J. Groeschel, C.F.R.

9 | *Trust Without Reservation*

When God becomes our guide he insists that we trust him without reservations and put aside all nervousness about his guidance. We are sent along the path he has chosen for us, but we cannot see it, and nothing we have read is any help to us....

God's activity can never be anything but good, and does not need to be reformed or controlled....

If we wish to live according to the Gospel, we must abandon ourselves simply and completely to the action of God. Jesus Christ is its source. He "is the same today as he was yesterday and as he will be forever" (Heb. 13:8).

—*Fr. Jean-Pierre de Caussade*

10 | *Rest a While*

Come now, insignificant man, fly for a moment from your affairs, escape for a little while from the tumult of your thoughts. Put aside now your weighty cares and leave your wearisome toils. Abandon yourself for a little to God and rest for a little while in him. Enter into the inner chamber of your soul, shut out everything save God and what can be of help in your quest for him and having locked the door seek him out. Speak now, my whole heart, speak now to God: "I seek your countenance, O Lord, your countenance I seek." Come then, Lord my God, teach my heart where and how to seek you, where and how to find you.

—*St. Anselm*

11 | *Remember*

When you lie down on your bed, remember with
thanksgiving the blessings and the providence of God.
—*St. Antony the Great*

12 | *He Knows What He Is About*

Therefore I will trust Him. Whatever, wherever I am, I
can never be thrown away. If I am in sickness, my sickness may serve Him; in perplexity, my perplexity may
serve Him; if I am in sorrow, my sorrow may serve Him.
My sickness, or perplexity, or sorrow may be necessary
causes of some great end, which is quite beyond us. He
does nothing in vain; He may prolong my life, He may
shorten it; He knows what He is about. He may take
away my friends, He may throw me among strangers,
He may make me feel desolate, make my spirits sink,
hide the future from me—still He knows what He is
about.

O Adonai, O Ruler of Israel, You who guided Joseph
like a flock, O Emmanuel, O Sapientia, I give myself
to You, I trust You wholly. You are wiser than I—more
loving to me than I myself. Fulfill Your high purposes
in me whatever they be—work in and through me.
—*Bl. Cardinal John Henry Newman*

13 | *He Holds You*

I do not pray that you may be delivered from your pains, but I pray earnestly to God that He would give you strength and patience to bear them as long as He pleases. Comfort yourself with Him who holds you fastened to the cross. He will loose you when He thinks fit. Happy those who suffer with Him…seek from Him the strength to endure as much, and as long, as He shall judge to be necessary for you…Continue then always with God; it is the only support and comfort for your affliction.

—Brother Lawrence

14 | *The Way of Trust*

[A person] will do what he can to change the unpleasant things he finds in himself, but he will discover quite a bit that can't be called beautiful and yet will be nearly impossible to change. As a result he will slowly become small and humble, increasingly patient and tolerant toward the specks in his brothers' eyes, now that he has so much trouble with the beam in his own. Eventually, he'll be able to look at himself in the unblinking light of the divine presence and learn to entrust himself to the power of the divine mercy.

—St. Teresa Benedicta of the Cross

15 | *Learning to Love*
The truth is that we cannot remain prisoners of the past;
people need a sort of "healing of the memories" so that
past evils will not come back again. This does not mean
forgetting past events; it means reexamining them with a
new attitude and learning precisely from the experience
of suffering that only love can build upwards, whereas
hatred produces only devastation and ruin.

—*Pope John Paul II*

16 | *The Gift of Song*
And then softly, to his own surprise, there at the vain
end of his long journey and his grief, moved by what
thought in his heart he could not tell, Sam began
to sing.

—*J.R.R. Tolkien*

17 | *Everlasting Joy*
Suffering is transient for those who are to be saved, and
will ultimately vanish completely. It is not God's will
therefore that we should grieve and sorrow over our
present sufferings, but rather that we should leave them
at once, and keep ourselves in his everlasting joy.

—*St. Julian of Norwich*

18 | *God Does Not Change*
Let nothing disturb you,
Let nothing frighten you,
Though all things pass
God does not change.
Patience wins all things.
But he lacks nothing
Who possesses God;
For God alone suffices.

—*St. Teresa of Avila*

19 | *The Virtue of the Cross*
Why, then, do you dread to take His Cross, since it is the very way to the kingdom of heaven, and there is no other way? In the Cross is health, in the Cross is life; in the Cross is the fullness of heavenly sweetness; in the Cross is strength of mind, joy of spirit, height of virtue, full perfection of all holiness, and there is no help for the soul, or hope of everlasting life, save through the virtue of the Cross.

Take, therefore, your cross and follow Jesus, and you shall go to life everlasting.

—*Fr. Thomas à Kempis*

20 | *The House of Love*

Why is there no reason to fear any longer? Jesus himself answers this question succinctly when he approaches his frightened disciples walking on the lake: "It is I. Do not be afraid" (John 6:20). The house of love is the house of Christ, the place where we can think, speak, and act in the way of God—not in the way of a fear-filled world. From this house the voice of love keeps calling out: "Do not be afraid…come and follow me…see where I live …go out and preach the good news…the kingdom of God is close at hand…there are many rooms in my Father's house. Come…take for your heritage the Kingdom prepared for you since the foundation of the world."

The house of love is not simply a place in the afterlife, a place in heaven beyond this world. Jesus offers us this house right in the midst of our anxious world.

—*Fr. Henri Nouwen*

21 | *The Hope in Our Hearts*

We are not the sum of our weaknesses and failures; we are the sum of the Father's love for us and our real capacity to become the image of his Son.

—*Pope John Paul II*

22 | *Invoking the Name*

Does one of us feel sad? Let the name of Jesus come into his heart... Does someone fall into sin? Does his despair even urge him to suicide? Let him but invoke this life-giving name and his will to live will be at once renewed. The hardness of heart that is our common experience, the apathy that bred of indolence, bitterness of mind, repugnance for the things of the spirit—have they ever failed to yield in presence of that saving name? ... And where is the man, who terrified and trembling before impending peril, has not been suddenly filled with courage and rid of fear by calling on the strength of that name? Where is the man who tossed on the rolling seas of doubt, did not quickly find certitude by recourse to the clarity of Jesus' name? Was ever a man so discouraged, so beaten down by afflictions, to whom the sound of this name did not bring new resolve? In short, for all the ills and disorders to which flesh is heir, this name is medicine.

—*St. Bernard of Clairvaux*

23 | *A Little Twig*

My daughter, all your miseries have been consumed in the flame of My love, like a little twig thrown into a roaring fire.

—*Words of Jesus to St. Faustina Kowalska*

24 | *The Answer Is a Person*

The solution to troubles—even the darkest and most severe troubles—does not lie in understanding *why* they happened. We creatures cannot unravel the mysteries of good and evil. The solution is to cling to God in hope and gratitude. He is always with us.

How do we cling to God? The answer is not a program, an insight, or an idea. It's a person—Jesus. We can cling to Jesus because he knows the most terrible trouble from the inside out....

Here is a leader we can follow into our afflictions. We can take up our cross and follow him because he has been there before us.

—*Fr. Michael Scanlan, T.O.R.*

25 | *The Way to Heaven*

What does it matter to you whether Jesus wishes to guide you to Heaven by way of the desert or by the fields, so long as you get there by one way or the other? Put away any excessive worrying which results from the trials by which the good God has desired to test you; and if this is not possible, resign yourself to the Divine will.

—*St. Padre Pio*

26 | *Safely Through the Storm*

We shall steer safely through every storm, as long as our heart is right, our intention fervent, our courage steadfast, and our trust fixed in God.

—*St. Francis de Sales*

27 | *In the Hands of the Sculptor*

It is true that a canvas simply and blindly offered to the brush feels at each moment only the stroke of the brush. It is the same with a lump of stone. Each blow from the hammering of the sculptor's chisel makes it feel—if it could—as if it were being destroyed. As blow after blow descends, the stone knows nothing of how the sculptor is shaping it. All it feels is a chisel chopping away at it, cutting it and mutilating it…. We might ask it: "What do you think is happening to you?" And it might answer: "Don't ask me. All I know is that I must stay immovable in the hands of the sculptor, and I must love him and endure all he inflicts on me to produce the figure he has in mind. He knows how to do it. As for me, I have no idea what he is doing, nor do I know what he will make of me. But what I do know is that his work is the best possible. It is perfect. I welcome each blow of his chisel as the best thing that could happen to me, although, if I'm to be truthful, I feel that every one of these blows is ruining me, destroying me and disfiguring me. But I remain unconcerned. I concentrate on the present moment, think only of my duty, and suffer all that this master sculptor inflicts on me without knowing his purpose or fretting about it."

Yes, you frank and precious souls, leave to God what is his business and carry on peacefully with your work. Be quite sure that whatever happens to your spiritual life or to your activities in the world is always for the best. Let God act, and abandon yourself to him.

—*Fr. Jean-Pierre de Caussade*

28 | *You Alone*

O Lord, what is the trust that I can have in this life, or what is my greatest solace among all things under heaven? Is it not You, my Lord God, whose mercy is without measure? Where have things been well with me without You, and when have things not been well with me if You were present? I would rather be poor with You than rich without You. I would rather be with You a pilgrim in this world, than without You to be in heaven. Where You are is heaven, and where You are not is both death and hell. You are to me all that I desire, and therefore it is fitting for me to cry to You and heartily to pray to You. I have nothing save You to trust in that can help me in my necessity, for You are my hope, You are my trust, You are my comfort, and You are my most faithful helper in every need.

—*Fr. Thomas à Kempis*

29 | *Pruning Bears Fruit*

God calls me to more. God wants to prune me. A pruned vine does not look beautiful, but during harvest time it produces much fruit. The greatest challenge is to continue to recognize God's pruning hand in my life. Then I can avoid resentment and depression and become even more grateful that I am called upon to bear even more fruit than I thought I could. Suffering then becomes a way of purification and allows me to rejoice in its fruits with deep gratitude and without pride.

—*Fr. Henri Nouwen*

30 | *Purified Like Gold*

I would like to make everyone understand the great grace that God, in His mercy, bestows when He sends suffering, especially suffering devoid of consolation. Then indeed the soul is purified like gold in the furnace; without knowing it, it becomes radiant and is set free to take flight to its Good.

—*St. Paul of the Cross*

31 | *Confidence in God*

The supreme test…of our confidence in God lies, perhaps, in those moments of complete inner darkness in which we feel as though we are forsaken by God. Our heart feels blunt; our prayers for strength and inspiration sound hollow; they seem plainly to be of no avail; wherever we look, our glance perceives but our impotence and, as it were, an impenetrable wall separating us from God.…

It is in such moments, when we are most tempted to part with our confidence in God, that we need it most. An ardent belief in His love; a steadfast conviction that *He* is near to us even though *we* are, or imagine ourselves to be, far away from Him; an unbroken awareness that "He hath first loved us, and sent His Son to be a propitiation for our sins"—these must carry us across the chasms of darkness and lend us strength to let ourselves blindly fall into His arms.

—*Dietrich von Hildebrand*

32 | *A Good Start*

A first essential setting for learning hope is prayer. When no one listens to me any more, God still listens to me. When I can no longer talk to anyone or call upon anyone, I can always talk to God. Where there is no longer anyone to help me deal with a need or expectation that goes beyond the human capacity for hope, he can help me. When I have been plunged into complete solitude, if I pray I am never totally alone.

—*Pope Benedict XVI*

33 | *A New Perspective*

The reality of suffering is ever before our eyes and often in the body, soul, and heart of each of us. Pain has always been a great riddle of human existence. However, ever since Jesus redeemed the world by His passion and death, a new perspective has been opened: through suffering one can grow in self-giving and attain the highest degree of love because of Him who "loved us and gave himself up for us."

—*Pope John Paul II*

34 | *The Lord Knows My Fear*

Today, O Lord, I felt intense fear. My whole being seemed to be invaded by fear. No peace, no rest; just plain fear: fear of mental breakdown, fear of living the wrong life, fear of rejection and condemnation, and fear of you....

You, O Lord, have also known fear. You have been deeply troubled; your sweat and tears were the signs of your fear. Make my fear, O Lord, part of yours, so that it will lead me not to darkness but to the light, and will give me a new understanding of the hope of your cross.

—*Fr. Henri Nouwen*

35 | *Go to God*

[I]f some great misfortune should actually happen, instead of wasting time in complaint or self-pity, go throw yourself at once at the feet of your Savior and implore His grace to bear your trial with fortitude and patience. A man who has been badly wounded does not, if he is wise, chase after his assailant, but makes straight for a doctor who may save his life....

So go to God, but go at once.

—*St. Claude de la Colombière*

36 | *A Firm Hand*

Let us then as Christians rejoice that we see around us on every hand the decay of the institutions and instruments of power, see intimations of empires falling to pieces, money in total disarray, dictators and parliamentarians alike nonplused by the confusion and conflicts which encompass them. For it is precisely when every earthly hope has been explored and found wanting, when every possibility of help from earthly sources has been sought and is not forthcoming, when every recourse this world offers, moral as well as material, has been explored to no effect, when in the shivering cold the last [log] has been thrown on the fire and in the gathering darkness every glimmer of light has finally flickered out, it's then that Christ's hand reaches out sure and firm.

—Malcolm Muggeridge

37 | *Lord, to Be With You*

Lord, it is good for me to suffer, so long as you are with me, better than to reign without you, to feast without you, to boast without you. Lord, it is better for me to embrace you in tribulation, to have you with me in the furnace, than to be without you, even in heaven. What is there for me in heaven, and what have I desired save you on the earth? Gold is tried in the furnace, and just men in the test of tribulation. Lord, there you are, there with them: there you stand in the midst of those who are gathered in your name, as you stood once with the three young men. Why are we afraid, why do we delay, why do we flee from this furnace? The fire rages, but the Lord is with us in tribulation. If God is with us, who can be against us? Furthermore, if he rescues us, who can snatch us out of his hand? Who can take us from his grasp? Finally, if he glorifies us, who can make us inglorious? If he glorifies us, who can humiliate us?

—*St. Bernard of Clairvaux*

38 | *The Way*

Therefore stay close to Christ if you want to be secure. You will not be able to stray from the way since he is the way.

—*St. Thomas Aquinas*

39 | *Make Yourself at Home*

It is just as well to make yourself at home with the sufferings that Jesus is pleased to send you, as you must always live with them. In this way, when you are least expecting to be liberated from them, Jesus, who cannot bear to keep you long in affliction, will come and relieve you and comfort you, giving you new courage.

—*St. Padre Pio*

40 | *A Long Trial*

This time the trial has been long. Perhaps—and without the perhaps—you haven't borne it well so far, for you were still seeking human consolations. But your Father God has torn them out by the roots so as to leave you no other refuge but him.

—*St. Josemaría Escrivá*

41 | *Safe Passage*

If I try by myself to swim across the ocean of this world, the waves will certainly engulf me. In order to survive I must climb aboard a ship made of wood; this wood is the Cross of Christ. Of course, even on board ship there will be dangerous tempests and perils from the sea of this world. But God will help me remain on board the ship and arrive safely at the harbor of eternal life.

—*St. Augustine*

42 | *Never Alone*

We may feel miles away from peace, we may have no inkling as to how the present situation can ever come right, but by voluntarily surrendering and by exercising trust we *know* that we are not being left alone in our misery and that we can expect eventually to "be supremely happy with him in the next life."

—*Dom Hubert van Zeller*

43 | *Everything Is Grace*

If we love God, we will understand that everything is grace, that Job's sores were grace, that Job's abandonment was grace, that even Jesus' abandonment ("My God, my God, why hast Thou forsaken Me?") was grace. Even the delay of grace is grace. Suffering is grace. The cross is grace. The grave is grace....

...Our struggle against suffering and every form of evil, physical and spiritual, is part of God's will for us and part of our growing.

—*Peter Kreeft*

44 | *Waiting*

Waiting and patience are necessary if we are to fulfill what we have begun to be, and to receive, through God's unfailing help, what we hope for and believe.

—*St. Cyprian of Carthage*

45 | *The Place of "What's This?"*

And one is led out into the desert, into the place of "What's this?" the place where we are fed and tended in a way that eludes our comprehension, precisely so that we may learn to live by faith, by trust in the living God. And so learn not to be God ourselves.

—*Fr. Simon Tugwell, O.P.*

46 | *Most Loyal Friend*

What more do we want than to have at our side a friend so loyal that he will never desert us when we are in trouble or in difficulties, as worldly friends do?

—*St. Teresa of Avila*

47 | *You Can't Please Everybody*

Don't allow yourself to be upset by what other people are saying about you. Let the world talk. All you need to be concerned about is doing the will of God. As for what people want, you can't please everybody, and it isn't worth the effort. One quiet moment in the presence of God will more than repay you for every bit of slander that will ever be leveled against you. You must learn to love other people without expecting friendship from them at all…. Just be sure that you see only God in them. They could do nothing to you without His permission. So, in the end, it is He that tests or blesses us, using them as we have need.

—*Bishop Francois de Salignac de La Mothe Fénelon*

48 | *No Turning Back*

No misfortune should distract us from this happiness and deep joy; for if anyone is anxious to reach a destination, the roughness of the road will not make him change his mind.

—*Pope St. Gregory the Great*

49 | *To Live by Faith*

He brings life out of the shadow of death, and when, with human weakness, we are afraid, faith, which sees good in all things and knows that all is for the best, remains full of a confident courage....

To live by faith is to live joyfully, to live with assurance, untroubled by doubts and with complete confidence in all we have to do and suffer at each moment by the will of God.

—*Fr. Jean-Pierre de Caussade*

50 | *The Night of Preparation*

A true dark night is accompanied by deep, painful longing for God. This is acutely present in Mother Teresa. One sign that it is an authentic dark night is that we don't in our aridity try to fill the emptiness with worldly or fleshly consolations but remain faithful in seeking God even in the pain of his apparent absence. The authentic dark night isn't an end in itself, but is intended to prepare us for an even greater union with and experience of God.

—*Ralph Martin*

51 | *The Purpose of the Dark Night*

Even though this *blessed night* darkens the spirit,
   it does so only to impart light in all things.
And even though it humbles us and reveals our miseries,
   it does so only to exalt us.
And even though it empties us of everything…
   it does so only that we may reach forward divinely
   to enjoy and to taste everything in heaven and on
      earth,
   while preserving a general freedom of spirit in all.
                 —*St. John of the Cross*

52 | *Our Help in Time of Need*

One thing alone I know—that according to our need, so will be our strength. One thing I am sure of, that the more the enemy rages against us, so much the more will the Saints in Heaven plead for us; the more fearful are our trials from the world, the more present to us will be our Mother Mary, and our good Patrons, and Angel Guardians; the more malicious are the devices of men against us, the louder cry of supplication will ascend from the bosom of the whole Church to God for us. We shall not be left orphans; we shall have within us the strength of the Paraclete, promised to the Church and to every member of it.

                 —*Bl. Cardinal John Henry Newman*

53 | *Opportunity Knocks*

Some people's lives are filled with more hardship than others. But make no mistake—every life's journey has some tough stretches. Everyone is tested, everyone brought to the line. There will be occasional bumps in the road, unpleasant surprises, irritating delays, annoying mistakes and accidents. There will be days when everything seems to go wrong. ("When sorrows come, they come not single spies, but in battalions," Shakespeare observes in *Hamlet*.) And there will be those moments when our whole world seems to be falling apart....

If met correctly, of course, most of the troubles we encounter in life become opportunities to know and add to the strength of our virtues. The blows of adversity can be the best chances for improvement. "The gem cannot be polished without friction, nor man perfected without trials," a Chinese proverb says....

The ultimate test, however, is not whether we finally reach [our] goal but how we conduct ourselves along the way. For sometimes the path is too steep to make it all the way to the top, and we must trust that the struggle itself was worth it and ready ourselves for new tests knowing, as the clergyman Henry Ward Beecher put it more than one hundred years ago, "We are always in the forge, or on the anvil; by trials God is shaping us for higher things."

—*William J. Bennett*

54 | *The Extremity of God's Love*
All things fail, but You, O Lord of them all, never fail.
…You seem, O Lord, to give extreme tests to those who
love You, but only that, in the extremity of their trials,
they may learn the greater extremity of Your love.

—*St. Teresa of Avila*

55 | *More Than We Can Ever Attain*
Young people can have the hope of a great and fully sat-
isfying love; the hope of a certain position in their pro-
fession, or of some success that will prove decisive for
the rest of their lives. When these hopes are fulfilled,
however, it becomes clear that they were not, in reality,
the whole. It becomes evident that man has need of a
hope that goes further. It becomes clear that only something infinite will suffice for him, something that will
always be more than he can ever attain.

—*Pope Benedict XVI*

56 | *Looking at the Present*

It is quite a mistake to trouble ourselves as to what I may still have to suffer. It is like meddling with God's work. We who run in the way of love must never allow ourselves to be disturbed by anything. *If I did not simply live from one moment to the next, it would be impossible for me to be patient;* but I look only at the present. I forget the past, and take good care not to forestall the future. *When we yield to discouragement or despair, it is usually because we think too much about the past and the future.*

—*St. Thérèse of the Child Jesus*

57 | *The Great Reward*

Only a little more confidence in God. A little more patience. And the end will come, and past weary years will seem as nothing.

Then will arrive the moment of reunion, and all will be amply compensated and repaid, principal and interest.

—*St. Théophane Vénard*

58 | *Be Not Afraid*

[W]hen terror holds us in its grip, hope is often born. Darkness yields to light. A Savior has been born, the Lord Christ himself, for "God so loved the world as to give His only begotten Son; that whosoever believeth in him may not perish, but may have life everlasting" (John 3:16).

Do not be afraid. We need never be alone. Every burden carried by us is also shared by him. "Give me your burden," he says, "and I will make it mine." He will not always lift the burden from us, but being his, too, it is lighter now and easier.

We do not understand why we are fallen and sinful, burdened and wounded. He does not will our sadnesses or our pain. He wants us to know his goodness and to trust, to find his love and rejoice.

—*Cardinal Basil Hume*

59 | *The Gentle Touch*

How amazing and how pitiful it is that the weakness and woundedness of the soul are such that it experiences the gentle and light hand of God so heavy and contrary to it. The Lord only touches it, and does so mercifully without pressing it down or weighing upon it. God does this in order to pour out his graces upon the soul, not to punish it.

—*St. John of the Cross*

60 | *For Those We Love*

It is comparatively easy not to be absorbed in our own suffering, but the suffering of those we love is apt to become a constant and unhappy obsession, against which we must struggle: first by prayer, confiding those we love to God in complete filial abandonment, then by work, and also by an occupation chosen outside the center of our thoughts and affections. Finally, by doing good to others, we can try to forget a little of our dear ones' burdens, which are a thousand times more painful than the ones we carry alone.

—*Servant of God Elisabeth Leseur*

61 | *Search for Him*

Seek Jesus. Let your life be a continual, sincere search for Him, without ever tiring, without ever abandoning the undertaking, even though darkness should fall on your spirit, temptations beset you, and grief and incomprehension wring your heart. These are the things that are part of life here below; they are inevitable, but they can also be beneficial because they mature our spirit. We must never turn back, even if it should seem to you that the light of Christ is fading. On the contrary, continue seeking with renewed faith and greater generosity.

—*Pope John Paul II*

62 | *Standing on the Rock*

The waves are many and the surging sea dangerous. But we are not afraid we may be drowned. For we are standing on the rock. Let the sea rage as it will, it cannot split the rock asunder. Though the waves tower on high, they cannot overwhelm the boat of Jesus. What, pray, are we afraid of? Death? "For me life is Christ, and death gain." But tell me, is it exile? "The earth is the Lord's, and all it contains." Is it the loss of property? "We brought nothing into the world. It is certain we can take nothing out of it." The terrors of the world I despise, its treasures I deem laughable. I am not afraid of poverty, I do not long for wealth. I do not dread death.

—*St. John Chrysostom*

63 | *Whatever You Want of Me*

I will no longer look back, but do willingly, simply, humbly, and bravely the duties that come from the circumstances in which I find myself, as your will. To do quickly. To do everything. To do it well. To do it joyfully—whatever you want of me right now, even if it is beyond my strength, even if it asks my life. Finally, at this last hour.

—*Pope Paul VI*

64 | *On the Night of Hugo*

In the darkness of that night—
That darkness on every side of me,
Above, around and within me—
In that darkness that brought uprooting
And pruning so far beyond the wildest
Images I had known,
In that darkness I sought You, Lord,
And You came
Not in any way I could foreknow
Nor in a way I could imagine.

You found me, Lord,
In my knowledge of my nothingness.

In that nothingness, my Lord,
Now am I content to be
For now I perceive
That Your Love has ever sheltered me
From grievous harms on every side of me
In every place, in every time.

It is this perceiving, Lord, that
Now impels me seeking, ever searching
Ever thirsting, longing, yearning
For that Center that is
Thine own most gracious Heart
Beyond all space and time.

—*Fr. Aidan Mullaney*

65 | *On the Verge*

I will not mistrust [God], though I feel myself weakening and on the verge of being overcome with fear…. I trust he shall place his holy hand on me and in the stormy seas hold me up from drowning.

—*St. Thomas More*

66 | *Love Only Eternal Life*

Because we cannot endure perpetually the hardships of life, we seek rest in some earthly thing. It may be our house, our family, our children, a little farm, an orchard, or a book we have published. God allows us to suffer tribulations even in these innocent delights in order that we may love only life eternal. Otherwise, as travelers going to their country, we might choose the inn—this world—instead of our true home: eternal life.

—*St. Augustine*

67 | *Jesus! Save Me!*

Remember how Peter walked over the turmoil of the deep sea and strong winds toward Jesus. The heart of Jesus is more powerful than all our pain and fear. Do not ever doubt the truth of this. But do not let that truth leave you complacent as you sink sweetly beneath the waves! Rather, cry out, "Jesus! Save me! Out of my depths I cry, depths I myself do not know, but which you do!" (see Psalm 130).

—*Msgr. Peter Magee*

68 | *We Can Do It*

Jesus' extreme love impels us to live every suffering—as much as we are given—like him and in him.

And we can do it.

We can if, in each personal suffering and in those of others, we recognize a shadow of his infinite suffering, an aspect, an expression of his. Then, each time this suffering shows itself, we do not distance ourselves from it, but accept it fully as if we were accepting him. Forgetting ourselves, we cast our whole being into what God asks of us in the present moment, in the neighbor he places before us, motivated only by love. Then, very often we will see our sufferings vanish as if by some magic, and only love remains in the soul.

—*Cardinal Francis Xavier Nguyen Van Thuan*

69 | *The Cup of Joy*

Joys are hidden in sorrows! I know this from my own times of depression. I know it from living with people with mental handicaps. I know it from looking into the eyes of patients, and from being with the poorest of the poor. We keep forgetting this truth and become overwhelmed by our own darkness. We easily lose sight of our joys and speak of our sorrows as the only reality there is.

We need to remind each other that the cup of sorrow is also the cup of joy, that precisely what causes us sadness can become the fertile ground for gladness. Indeed, we need to be angels for each other, to give each other strength and consolation. Because only when we fully realize that the cup of life is not only a cup of sorrow but also a cup of joy will we be able to drink it.

—*Fr. Henri Nouwen*

70 | *Run to the Father*

"Pray! Run to the Father!" God is waiting for His child
to come so that He can help him. Let us beg the Father
for help and take refuge in His strong arms, which will
carry us through. If we practice doing so now, we will
also turn to Him in time of persecution. When too
exhausted and pain-ridden to formulate long prayers, we
only have to say, "My Father, I trust You!" Let us say this
over and over again. It is a powerful prayer and will
bring us help, for we receive according to our trust.
Either God will save us from our plight or we will experience His loving presence so wonderfully that the hor-
rors about us will fade away.

—*Mother Basilea Schlink*

71 | *Moment by Moment*

It is a great gift to be able to be peaceful when you are
facing situations that do not seem to change. Bear all the
uncomfortable and inconvenient things about your current situation. Look at them as exercises that God has
designed for your growth. He is teaching you to bear
difficult situations without being depressed. Your emo-
tions may be low, but your inner man is being upheld.
This peace is all the more precious when there is no
earthly reason to have it.

It is wonderful to be willing to accept all situations,
no matter how difficult. It is good to never say, "This is
all too much for me, I cannot bear it." Depend on the
Almighty. God's hand holds you. Do not try to look too
far ahead, but merely live moment by moment before

God. Yield to God with a heart full of trust. The more God loves you, the less He spares you. Accept what comfort He gives you. Live to do His will alone.

—*Bishop Francois de Salignac de La Mothe Fénelon*

72 | *The Flood of Divine Life*
There is nothing more free than a heart which sees only the life of God in the most deadly perils and troubles. Even when it is a question of drinking poison, standing in the breach during a battle, or slaving for the plague-stricken, it finds in its circumstances a veritable plenitude of divine life, not given to them by drops, but in floods which overwhelm and engulf the soul in an instant.

If an army were animated by the same ideals, it would be invincible, because the moving power of faith lifts and enlarges the heart above and beyond anything the senses can experience.

—*Fr. Jean-Pierre de Caussade*

73 | *God's Providence*
In the winter, seeing a tree stripped of its leaves, and considering that within a little time the leaves would be renewed and after that the flowers and fruit appear, Brother Lawrence received a high view of the Providence and Power of God, which has never been erased from his soul.

—*Brother Lawrence*

Becoming Real

"Real isn't how you are made," said the Skin Horse. "It's a thing that happens to you. When a child loves you for a long, long time, not just to play with, but REALLY loves you, then you become Real."

"Does it hurt?" asked the Rabbit.

"Sometimes," said the Skin Horse, for he was always truthful. "When you are Real you don't mind being hurt."

"Does it happen all at once, like being wound up," he asked, "or bit by bit?"

"It doesn't happen all at once," said the Skin Horse. "You become. It takes a long time. That's why it doesn't often happen to people who break easily, or have sharp edges, or who have to be carefully kept. Generally, by the time you are Real, most of your hair has been loved off, and your eyes drop out and you get loose in the joints and very shabby. But these things don't matter at all, because once you are Real you can't be ugly, except to people who don't understand."

"I suppose *you* are Real?" said the Rabbit. And then he wished he had not said it, for he thought the Skin Horse might be sensitive. But the Skin Horse only smiled.

"The Boy's Uncle made me Real," he said. "That was a great many years ago; but once you are Real you can't become unreal again. It lasts for always."

The Rabbit sighed. He thought it would be a long time before this magic called Real happened to him. He longed to become Real, to know what it felt like; and yet the idea of growing shabby and losing his eyes and whiskers was rather sad. He wished that he could become it without these uncomfortable things happening to him.

—*Margery Williams,* The Velveteen Rabbit

75 | *Suffering Creates Life*

Our suffering works mysteriously, first in ourselves by a kind of renewal, and also in others, perhaps far away, without our ever knowing what we are accomplishing. Suffering is an action. Christ on the cross has perhaps done more for humanity than Christ speaking and acting in Galilee or Jerusalem. Suffering creates life; it transforms all that it touches.

—*Servant of God Elisabeth Leseur*

76 | *Renewing Hope*

We need difficulties to enliven our hope, patience to test it, a community to support it, and God to direct it. We purify our hope as we separate what is superficial from what is essential, what is fleeting from what is lasting....

...The loss of hope—despair—is ultimately the refusal to be oneself and to accept one's destiny. It is a preference for immediacies and illusions over authenticity and eternity. To renew one's fundamental hope, one must "turn around" and face what is most real and most important and embrace it with one's whole being.

—*Donald De Marco*

77 | *All for the Good*

If we have any natural defect, either in mind or body, let us not grieve and be sorry for ourselves.

Who is there that ever receives a gift and tries to make bargains about it? Let us, then, return God thanks for what, through a pure act of His Goodness, He has bestowed upon us, and let us be content with the manner in which He has treated us. Who can tell whether, if we had had a larger share of ability or stronger health, we should not have possessed them to our destruction?

—*St. Alphonsus Liguori*

78 | *Grace in Temptation*

Therefore, we shall not despair when we are tempted, but shall the more fervently pray to God, that of His infinite goodness and fatherly pity He may promise to help us in every need; and that, according to the saying of St. Paul, He may so go before us with His grace in every temptation that we may be able to bear it. Let us, then, humble ourselves under the strong hand of Almighty God, for He will save and exalt all who are here meek and lowly in spirit.

—*Fr. Thomas à Kempis*

79 | *The One Thing to Fear*
There is only one thing to be feared … only one trial
and that is sin. …. All the rest is beside the point,
whether you talk of plots, feuds, betrayals, slanders,
abuses, confiscations of property, exile, swords, open seas
or universal war. Whatever they may be, they are all
fugitive and perishable. They touch the mortal body but
wreak no harm on the watchful soul.

—*St. John Chrysostom*

80. | *My Present Moment*
If I look at the future, I am full of fear,
but why go forward into the future?
Only the present moment is dear to me,
because perhaps the future will not lodge in my soul.

The past is not within my power
to change, correct, or add something.
Neither the wise not the prophets were able to do this.
I trust therefore to God that which regards my past.

O present moment, you belong to me completely;
I desire to use you as much as it is within my power….

Therefore, trusting in your mercy,
I go forward in life as a child,
and every day I offer to you my heart
enflamed with love for your greater glory.

—*St. Faustina Kowalska*

81 | *God's Steady Finger*

None of us are wise enough to properly apportion grace and suffering. We cannot see the extent of our future trials, nor of the vast supplies of which God is storing up in us so that we can meet them. And because we cannot see those future trials, nor the grace that will be needed for them, we are tempted to become discouraged and despondent in our present situations. We see our trials rolling in toward us like great, overpowering, ocean waves. Our hearts fail us with fear at the prospect of drowning. We do not see that we stand within the point at which God, with a steady finger, has drawn the boundary line. Beyond that line the waves cannot pass.

—*Bishop Francois de Salignac de La Mothe Fénelon*

82 | *Endurance*

Our endurance must go beyond confessing the name of Christian when punishment by sword and fire is threatened. We must also endure such temptations as differences in customs, insults from those who disobey God, and the barbs of wicked tongues. In fact, no occupation is without its dangers. But who will guide the ship through the waves if the pilot quits his post? Who will guard against wolves if the shepherd does not watch? Or who will drive away the robber if sleep removes the watchman from the lookout point?

Stick by the work entrusted to you and the task you have undertaken.

Observe justice and show mercy.

Hate the sins, not the sinner.

Strengthen the weak and correct the proud.

Even if tribulation brings us more than we can endure, let us not be afraid as if we were resisting in our own strength.

—*St. Braulio of Saragossa*

83 | *The Greatest Lie*

Despair is the victory of the devil in a mind that freely embraces it. Despair has believed the diabolical gospel that evil is stronger than good, that Jesus was a fake and a failure and that good is the illusion of the weak and naïve. Despair is the greatest lie of the greatest liar. Despair is the sin of ceasing to hope for personal salvation from God, for help in attaining it or for the forgiveness of one's sins. Despair is contrary to God's goodness, to his justice and to his mercy, for he is faithful to his promises.

Without compromise we must send thoughts of despair back to whence they came: to hell. We need never despair of the forgiveness of God. His mercy in Jesus is our ultimate hope. It destroys even despair and beats evil's lying claims.

—*Msgr. Peter Magee*

84 | *The School of Love*

For suffering is a school of love. And our activity will be the greater when…we are sad, weary, and desolate as a result of failure and abandoned by all, despised and mocked like Jesus on the Cross; if we only pray with all our might for our persecutors and desire by all means to lead them through the Immaculata to God. We must not feel hurt if we do not see the fruits of our labor. Maybe it is the will of God that they be harvested only after our death.

—*St. Maximilian Kolbe*

85 | *Fly to Jesus*

In every disappointment, great or small, let your dear heart fly direct to Him, to your Savior, throwing yourself into His arms for refuge in every pain and sorrow; He will never leave you nor forsake you.

—*St. Elizabeth Ann Seton*

86 | *Strengthened by Faith*

It may happen that for a certain time a man is illumined and refreshed by God's grace, and then this grace is withdrawn. This makes him inwardly confused and he starts to grumble; instead of seeking through steadfast prayer to recover his assurance of salvation, he loses patience and gives up. He is like a beggar who receives alms from the palace, and feels put out because he was not asked inside to dine with the king. "Blessed are those who have not seen and yet have come to believe." (Jn 20:29) Blessed also are those who, when grace is withdrawn, find no consolation in themselves, but only continuing tribulation and thick darkness, and yet do not despair; but, strengthened by faith, they endure courageously, convinced that they do indeed see him who is invisible.

—*St. John of Karpathos*

87 | *Help for the Heart*

You have not suffered or do not suffer in vain. Pain matures you in spirit, purifies you in heart, gives you a real sense of the world and of life, enriches you with goodness, patience, and endurance, and—hearing the Lord's promise reecho in your heart: "Blessed are those who mourn, for they shall be comforted" (Mt. 5:4)— gives you the sense of deep peace, perfect joy, and happy hope. Succeed, therefore, in giving a Christian value to your suffering, succeed in sanctifying your suffering with constant and generous hope in him who comforts and gives strength. I want you to know that you are not alone, or separated, or abandoned in your Via Crucis; beside you, each one of you, is the Blessed Virgin, who considers you her most beloved children.

—*Pope John Paul II*

88 | *A Great Teacher*

The suffering of adversity does not degrade you but exalts you. Human tribulation teaches you; it does not destroy you. The more we are afflicted in this world, the greater is our assurance for the next. The more we sorrow in the present, the greater will be our joy in the future.

—*St. Isidore of Seville*

89 | *There Is Hope*

Hope should allay fear; it should kill fear.... Christ has risen; and every moment can become the moment of beginning again....

In our search for reality, in our running from fear, in all of those emotional problems, there is hope. Stretch out your hands and hope will come to you, and whatever seems hopeless will be filled with light....

We say that "perfect love casts out all fear." But do we believe it? It is a very good intellectual exercise to repeat that sentence to ourselves, or to write it out on paper. Then, perhaps, it will sink into our hearts. If we turn our faces to hope, and look hope "in the eye" as it were, then it becomes very simple; for hope holds love in the hollow of its hand....

Hope makes us see that our price has been the incarnation, life, death and resurrection of Christ. Hope is like an avalanche of sorts, or like a fire that enters into you and renews you.

—*Catherine de Hueck Doherty*

90 | *Contend for the Crown*
What Saint has ever won his crown without first contending for it?

—*St. Jerome*

91 | *Strong in Christ*
Christian love gives value and meaning to our existence even when infirmity and illness have compromised the integrity of the body. There is a life in us not conditioned by our physical state, but by the love we give. "You who are sick, you are strong like Jesus on the cross," exclaimed John Paul II one day. Yes, because our strength is in Christ, in Christ crucified and abandoned! It is when we are weak that we are strong.

I touched this reality in prison. When I lived through times of extreme physical and moral suffering, I thought of Jesus crucified. To the human eye, his life was a defeat, a disappointment, and a failure. Reduced to the most absolute immobility on the cross, he was no longer able to encounter people, to cure the sick, to teach.... However, in the eyes of God, that was the most important moment of his life, because it was then that he poured out his blood for the salvation of humanity.

—*Cardinal Francis Xavier Nguyen Van Thuan*

92 | *The Power to Turn*

We have seen how every soul—even if burdened with sin, enmeshed in vice, ensnared by the allurements of pleasure, a captive in exile, imprisoned in the body, caught in the mud, fixed in mire, bound to its members, a slave to care, distracted by business, afflicted with sorrow, wandering and straying, filled with anxious forebodings and uneasy suspicions, a stranger in a hostile land, and, according to the Prophet, sharing the defilement of the dead and counted with those who go down into hell—every soul, I say, standing thus under condemnation and without hope, has the power to turn and find it can not only breathe the fresh air of the hope of pardon and mercy, but also dare to aspire to the nuptials of the Word, not fearing to enter into alliance with God or to bear the sweet yolk of love with the King of angels.

—*St. Bernard of Clairvaux*

93 | *Lean on Him*

My hope is in Christ, who strengthens the weakest by His Divine help. I can do all in Him who strengthens me. His power is infinite, and if I lean on Him, it will be mine. His Wisdom is infinite, and if I look to Him for counsel, I shall not be deceived. His Goodness is infinite, and if my trust is stayed on Him, I shall not be abandoned.

—*Pope St. Pius X*

94 | *How We Suffer Matters*

From the outset we need to notice that suffering does not automatically improve a person. How and why we suffer matter immensely. If we become cynical and bitter in the afflictions that come our way, we are becoming worse, not better....

If, however, we respond to the blows and buffets of life in union with the Lord, in his suffering and death out of love for us, we grow rapidly in both holiness and joy.

—*Fr. Thomas Dubay, S.M.*

95 | *Always Give Thanks*

Whether I receive good or ill, I return thanks equally to God, who taught me always to trust him unreservedly.

—*St. Patrick of Ireland*

96 | *The Pillar of the Cloud*

Lead, kindly Light, through the encircling gloom;
    Lead Thou me on!
The night is dark, and I am far from home;
    Lead Thou me on!
Keep Thou my feet: I do not ask to see
The distant scene; one step enough for me.

I was not ever thus, nor prayed that Thou
    Shouldst lead me on.
I loved to choose and see my path; but now
    Lead Thou me on.
I loved the garish day, and, spite of fears,
Pride ruled my will; remember not past years.

So long Thy power hath blessed me, sure it still
    Will lead me on
O'er moor and fen, o'er crag and torrent, till
    The night is gone,
And in the morn those angel faces smile
Which I have loved long since, and lost awhile.

              —*Bl. Cardinal John Henry Newman*

97 | *Allow God to Mold You*

God doesn't want to discourage you or to spoil you.
Embrace the difficult circumstances you find yourself
in—even when you feel they will overwhelm you.
Allow God to mold you through the events He allows
to enter your life. This will make you flexible toward
the will of God. The events of life are like a furnace for
the heart. All your impurities are melted and your old
ways are lost.

—*Bishop Francois de Salignac de La Mothe Fénelon*

98 | *All Will Be Well*

And so our good Lord answered to all the questions and
doubts which I could raise, saying most comfortingly; I
may make all things well, and I can make all things well,
and I shall make all things well, and I will make all
things well; and you will see yourself that every kind of
thing will be well.

—*St. Julian of Norwich*

99 | *A Time for Prayer*

Times are bad! They have never been worse; for never before has a world civilization turned against the Divine Light…. But despite these facts, this is not the end of civilization; nor are we to be without hope. We have simply reached a moment in history where God is permitting us to feel our inadequacy, so long as we trust only in ourselves….

…This hope can be translated into victory in either of two ways: by prayerful rewaking our hearts, or by being brought within an inch of disaster, until from the depths of our insufficiency we cry out to the Goodness of God.

—*Bishop Fulton J. Sheen*

100 | *Get the Message?*

Sometimes when I wake up in the morning, I start to feel the pains of the day, and I say, "What in the world is this? How am I going to put up with this? Why did God let this happen to me?" Then I have to rewind the tape, so to speak, and ask, "What are my pains and aches telling me?" I am learning to respond with my mind and heart to what they are saying.

…First of all, they remind me that our life here doesn't last forever, and that everyone, even the healthiest person, is not going to be here for a very long time. Secondly, my pains tell me to be compassionate to others in pain, especially to the disabled…. My pains and limitations give me insight into what many people in the world have to suffer.

So God is communicating with us in the flow of events in our lives. He may be telling us to be patient, to be brave, to be courageous, to be kind, to be understanding, or to be forgiving. Whatever happens—even something sad and tragic—can send a message to us.

—*Fr. Benedict J. Groeschel, C.F.R.*

101 | *Transfiguration*

Our universe is a wounded universe, divided, suffering, with great despair and poverty, where there are many signs of death, division and hatred. But all of these signs of death are taken up in the Cross of Jesus and transfigured in the Resurrection. Our hope is that the winter of humanity will gradually be transformed to the bursting forth of love, for it is to this that we are called.

We will pass through the winter of suffering to the kingdom of God and rebirth....

...[W]e can say with hope, with confidence, with trust, "Come, Come Lord Jesus."

And he will answer, "Yes, I am coming soon. Yes, I am coming for you who are yearning for love. Be not afraid to love."

Come, Lord Jesus, Come.

—*Jean Vanier*

102 | *The Gift of Life*

The "gift of life," God's special gift, is no less beautiful when it is accompanied by illness or weakness, hunger or poverty, mental or physical handicaps, loneliness or old age. Indeed, at these times, human life gains extra splendor as it requires our special care, concern and reverence. It is in and through the weakest of human vessels that the Lord continues to reveal the power of his love.... At this grace-filled time of my life, as I experience suffering in union with Jesus our Lord and Redeemer, I offer gratitude to Almighty God for giving me the opportunity to continue my apostolate on behalf of life.

—*Archbishop Terence J. Cooke*

103 | *Keeping the Faith*

The killers were in the room where we'd watched the movie, overturning the furniture and calling out my name again and again. "We want Immaculée ... it's time to kill Immaculée."...

...I looked up and saw Jesus hovering above me in a pool of golden light, and his arms were reaching toward me....

Then Jesus spoke: "Mountains are moved with faith, Immaculée, but if faith were easy, all the mountains would be gone. Trust in me, and know that I will never leave you. Trust in me, and have no more fear. Trust in me, and I will save you. I shall put my cross upon this door, and they will not reach you. Trust in me, and you shall live."

—*Immaculée Ilibagiza*

104 | *The Real Treasure*

I am progressing along the path of life in my ordinary contentedly fallen and godless condition, absorbed in a merry meeting with my friends for the morrow or a bit of work that tickles my vanity today, a holiday or a new book, when suddenly a stab of abdominal pain that threatens serious disease, or a headline in the newspapers that threatens us all with destruction, sends this whole pack of cards tumbling down. At first I am overwhelmed, and all my little happinesses look like broken toys. Then, slowly and reluctantly, bit by bit, I try to bring myself into the frame of mind that I should be in at all times. I remind myself that all these toys were never intended to possess my heart, that my true good is in another world and my only real treasure is Christ.

—*C.S. Lewis*

105 | *Fill Me*

Overcome the finite with the infinite. Christ has created you because He wanted you. I know what you feel—terrible longing, with dark emptiness—and yet, He is the one in love with you. I do not know if you have seen these few lines before, but they fill and empty me:

"My God, my God, what is a heart
That thou should so eye and woo,
Pouring upon it all thy heart
As if thou had nothing else to do…?"

—*Bl. Teresa of Calcutta*

106 | *Tell God About It*

Go and find him when your patience and strength give out and you feel alone and helpless. Jesus is waiting for you in the chapel. Say to him, "Jesus, you know exactly what is going on. You are all I have, and you know all. Come to my help." And then go, and don't worry about how you are going to manage. That you have told God about it is enough. He has a good memory.

—*St. Jeanne Jugan*

107 | *You're Invited!*

When the Lord called you it was not to settle a score against you, nor to bring you to account for your sins. It was to save you, to forgive you, to offer you new life. In the gospel Jesus himself calls out to the whole human race: "Come to me, all you who are weary and over-burdened, and I will give you rest. Take my yoke on your shoulders and learn to imitate me, for I am meek and humble of heart; then you will find rest for your souls" (Matt. 11:28-29).

What an invitation! Come to me, all of you! Not just the powerful, the affluent, the educated, the strong, the healthy, the respectable; but also the weak, the poor, the underprivileged, the sick, the blind, the lame, the disabled, the hopeless, the abandoned. The Master makes no distinction between any of you; the good news is for everyone. Come to me, he says, all you who toil and groan under your burdens. He is interested especially in those who have squandered their lives, who are weighed down by their sins, who are filled with shame and no longer have any self respect. These are the ones he calls to himself, not to punish them, but to comfort their sorrows and ease their heavy load.

…Jesus promises to give you rest, by forgiving all your sins. All he asks is that you should come to him in faith.

—*St. John Chrysostom*

108 | *Confirming Faith*
On the day after Gaudete Sunday, December 16, 1963, [my mother] closed her eyes forever, but the radiance of her goodness has remained, and for me it has become more and more a confirmation of the faith by which she had allowed herself to be formed. I know of no more convincing proof for the faith than precisely the pure and unalloyed humanity that the faith allowed to mature in my parents and in so many other persons I have had the privilege to encounter.

—*Pope Benedict XVI*

109 | *Forgiveness*

Although angry feelings are natural and not in themselves sinful, they must be dealt with immediately and
not allowed to grow into the desire for revenge. Who are
we to seek to be avenged? If God chose to be avenged on
us, what would become of us? When your enemy comes
to you and asks your pardon, forgive him at once. Is this
so very difficult? I know it is hard to love someone when
he is actually attacking you, but is it so hard to love him
when he asks for forgiveness?…

…Why go on dragging your heart in the dust? Lift it
up to the Lord; believe in the power he has given you to
overcome yourself.

—*St. Augustine*

110 | *You've Got a Friend*

[L]et us think…of our Eucharistic Lord as a Friend, a
personal Friend. That title, after all, he claimed at the
Last Supper, "I have called you my friends"; using, prob-
ably, a Hebrew word which throws into relief the reci-
procity of human friendship, and thereby raising his
apostles to a kind of equality with himself. A shepherd
has so many sheep to look after, the doctor has so many
calls to make; your friend, when he comes to see you, is
at liberty, is at your disposal; he has "just dropped in."
And our Lord wants each of us to think of him in that
way; nor do we deceive ourselves if we think of him in
that way. Infinite Power, infinite Goodness, makes itself
infinitely available. Go to Communion in some little
country church, where you find yourself alone at the

altar rails, or go to Midnight Mass at Westminster Cathedral, and get sucked into the interminable queue…it makes no difference. In either case the sacred Host which you are destined to receive contains the whole of Christ, all meant for you. "Is my friend there?" he is saying; waiting for you, like the person who comes to meet you at a crowded terminus, looking out for that particular trick of walking, that particular way of holding yourself, which will single you out at a distance.

—*Msgr. Ronald Knox*

111 | *In the Hands of God*

I should know by this time that just because I *feel* that everything is useless and going to pieces and badly done and futile, it is not really that way at all. Everything is all right. It is in the hands of God. Let us abandon everything to Divine Providence.

—*Servant of God Dorothy Day*

112 | *No Fear*

An old man said, "Rising and walking and sitting, if
God is before your eyes, there is nothing with which the
Enemy can frighten you." If that thought abides in a
man, the strength of God shall cling to him.

—*The Desert Fathers*

113 | *Time Is Precious*

Why, dearest daughter, do you waste time in sadness
when time is so precious for the salvation of poor sinners? Get rid of your melancholy immediately. Don't
think any more about yourself. Do not indulge in so
many useless and dangerous reflections. Look ahead
always without ever looking back. Keep your gaze fixed
on the summit of perfection where Christ awaits you.

—*St. Frances Xavier Cabrini*

114 | *Our True Nature Revealed*

It is the extreme situation that best reveals what we are
essentially.

—*Flannery O'Connor*

115 | *The Mother's Answer*

Every woman who sees her child suffer, every woman who is separated from her child, every woman who must stand by helpless and see her child die, every woman who echoes the old cry, "Why, why, why *my* child?" has the answer from the Mother of Christ. She can look at the child through Mary's eyes, she can know the answer with Mary's mind, she can accept the suffering with Mary's will, she can love Christ in her child with Mary's heart—because Mary had made *her* a mother of Christ. It is Christ who suffers in her child; it is His innocence redeeming the world, His love saving the world.

—*Caryll Houselander*

116 | *Weathering Trials*

Long periods of well-being and comfort are in general dangerous to all. After such prolonged periods, weak souls become incapable of weathering any kind of trial. They are afraid of it. But strong souls in such periods are still able to mobilize and to show themselves, and to grow through this trial. Difficult trials and sufferings can facilitate the growth of the soul. In the West there is a widespread feeling…that if we highly value suffering this is masochism. On the contrary, it is a significant bravery when we respect suffering and understand what burdens it places on our soul.

—*Aleksandr Solzhenitsyn*

117 | *Rejoice in the Lord*

Rejoice in the Lord is said to those who love God, whose sins are forgiven, for whom a crown is laid up in heaven. This is a joy which nothing, which no man, as our Lord said to his Apostles, can take from you. Otherwise there are many who could not rejoice. Or might say: I am in such want that I am not sure of my next meal: how can I have any joy? Another says: I have just lost a child, a wife or a husband: how can I rejoice? Another is in sickness or pain or ill-used or slandered by unkind tongues. [These] things…are afflictions, they are sorrows so great that for a time they may take from the world all comfort, but they leave you your heavenly hope; of that comfort they cannot rob you…. It *is* a comfort that in spite of all, God loves us; it *is* a comfort that the sufferings of this present world (St. Paul says) are not worthy to be compared with the glory that is to be revealed in us; such thoughts *are* comfort…. Cheerfulness has ever been a mark of saints and good people. The Apostles went rejoicing, we read, after their scourging from the sight of the Council, because they were found worthy for the name of Jesus to suffer insult; the martyrs were cheerful…. Goodness, then,…is cheerful and no wonder, and if there are, as to be sure there are, some good people whose looks are commonly downcast and sad, that is a fault in them and they are not to be copied in it.

—*Fr. Gerard Manley Hopkins*

118 | *Are You Really Grateful?*

We cannot tell who is really grateful until we see whether he gives God hearty and sincere thanks in the midst of calamities.

—*St. Antiochus*

119 | *Refreshment*

Jesus calls out to people: Come to me, all who labor and are heavy laden. He promises what he alone can do. With him, my heart finds rest, more than can be found in all the wellness and fitness centers with their contributions to physical well-being. But he can relieve me of the burdens that weigh upon my soul. Of course, only under one condition: I must be prepared to learn from him and to take his yoke upon myself. Just as there is no physical fitness training without one's own participation, so Jesus can give us his "refreshment" only if we take on his "program." Compared with the troubles we are prepared to take upon ourselves for health and success, his "yoke" is actually not heavy. It is, quite simply: Love God and your neighbor.

—*Cardinal Christoph Schönborn*

120 | *Think of Eternity*

We have lost the measure which is eternity and so
earthly things and suffering easily depress our spirit.
Everything strikes us as being too heavy, too excessive....
On the contrary, while you are on earth and about to be
overwhelmed by tribulation, summon up your faith,...
(think the thoughts of eternity) and you will find the
weight of tribulation grow lighter, become bearable.
Let us say to ourselves, "What is this when set against
eternity?"

—Fr. Raniero Cantalamessa

The
Voices

Fr. Thomas à Kempis (circa 1380–1471), was a German monk and the author of *The Imitation of Christ*, one of the most widely read Christian spiritual books.

St. Anselm (circa 1033–1109), was an Italian Benedictine monk, philosopher, and archbishop of Canterbury. He is called the founder of Scholasticism and is known as the originator of the ontological argument for the existence of God.

St. Antiochus (died circa AD 110), was an early Christian martyr of Sardinia.

St. Antony the Great (251–356), was the central figure in the development of monasticism in Egypt and the Holy Land and a model and teacher for desert fathers of many generations.

St. Thomas Aquinas (circa 1225–1274), was a Dominican priest and one of the greatest theologians of all time. He is called the Angelic Doctor of the Church.

St. Augustine (354–430), was a bishop in North Africa, a prolific writer, and a doctor of the Church.

Pope Benedict XVI (Joseph Ratzinger) (1927—), began his pontificate in 2005. He is a scholar of the liturgy and previously served as the Vatican's chief doctrinal official.

William J. Bennett (1943—), is an American author and scholar who served as secretary of the Department of Education and director of the Office of National Drug Control Policy. He is an active spokesperson for conservatism and morality.

St. Bernard of Clairvaux (1090–1153), was a Cistercian abbot, mystic, spiritual writer, and doctor of the Church.

St. Braulio of Saragossa (590–651), was a noted scholar, writer, and advisor to the kings of Spain.

St. Frances Xavier Cabrini (1850–1917), the first American citizen to be canonized by the Church, was the foundress of the Missionary Sisters of the Sacred Heart. She was responsible for the establishment of nearly seventy orphanages, schools, and hospitals.

Fr. Raniero Cantalamessa (1934—), is a Franciscan Capuchin who was appointed preacher to the papal household in 1980 by Pope John Paul II. He is also a frequent speaker and prolific author.

Archbishop Terence J. Cooke (1921–1983), the cardinal archbishop of New York, led the United States Bishops Pro-Life Campaign and considered his work an apostolate on behalf of life. He died of cancer.

St. Cyprian of Carthage (circa 200–258), was a bishop in North Africa, a biblical scholar, and a martyr.

Servant of God Dorothy Day (1897–1980), was an American journalist, social activist, and devout Catholic convert. In the 1930s she helped establish the Catholic Worker Movement.

Fr. Jean-Pierre de Caussade (1675–1751), was a French priest of the Society of Jesus and a writer. He is best known for his work *Abandonment to Divine Providence*, which consists of letters addressed to those suffering different kinds of trial.

St. Claude de la Colombière (1641–1682), was a Jesuit priest who preached against Jansenism and advocated dedication to the

Sacred Heart of Jesus. He is considered a "white martyr" because of the imprisonment and abuse he suffered in defense of the faith.

Dr. Donald De Marco is a professor of philosophy at St. Jerome's University in Ontario, Canada. He has lectured and published extensively on subjects such as the virtues, bioethics, and John Paul II's Theology of the Body. He is the author of seventeen books and is married with five children.

St. Francis de Sales (1567–1622), was a bishop of Geneva and leader of the Catholic Reformation. His book *Introduction to the Devout Life* became a classic spiritual guide for living an authentic Christian life.

The desert fathers were hermits, ascetics, and monks who lived mainly in the Scetes Desert of Egypt, beginning around the third century. They were the first Christian hermits, abandoning the cities of the pagan world to live in solitude.

Catherine de Hueck Doherty (1896–1985), was a pioneer of social justice and foundress of the Madonna House Apostolate. She was also a prolific writer and a dedicated wife and mother.

Fr. Thomas Dubay, S.M. (1921—), a well-known retreat master and author, is an expert on the teachings and writings of the two mystical doctors of the Church, John of the Cross and Teresa of Avila.

St. Josemaría Escrivá (1902–1975), the founder of Opus Dei, was canonized by Pope John Paul II, who declared him to be "counted among the great witnesses of Christianity."

Francois de Salignac de La Mothe Fénelon (1651–1715), was a French bishop, theologian, and author.

Pope St. Gregory the Great (540–604), was known for his zeal. In spite of his many bodily sufferings, he is remembered for his magnificent contributions to the liturgy of the Mass and the Divine Office.

Fr. Benedict J. Groeschel, C.F.R., (1933—), is a retreat master, psychologist, well-known author, and one of the founders of the Franciscan Friars of the Renewal.

Fr. Gerard Manley Hopkins, S.J., (1844–1889), was an English poet, Roman Catholic convert, and Jesuit priest. His twentieth-century fame established him posthumously among the leading Victorian poets.

Caryll Houselander (1901–1954), was an artist and prolific author who enjoyed enormous literary success in the 1940s and 1950s.

Cardinal George Basil Hume, O.S.B., (1923–1999), was a monk for nearly sixty years before his appointment as archbishop of Westminster.

Immaculée Ilibagiza (1972—), is a speaker and author who survived the three-month slaughter of the Tutsi tribe in her native Rwanda in 1994. She tells her story of God's faithfulness in *Left to Tell: Discovering God Amidst the Rwandan Holocaust* (Hay House, 2007).

St. Isidore of Seville (circa 560–636), was a bishop, scholar, educator, liturgist, philosopher, and doctor of the Church.

St. Jerome (circa 342–420), was an early Church scholar who is credited with shaping the Latin version of the Bible.

St. John Chrysostom (circa 347–407), archbishop of Constantinople and a Church father, was known for his eloquence in preaching.

St. John of Karpathos was a seventh-century monk from the Greek island of Karpathos whose writings were aimed at offering encouragement to those tempted to abandon the monastic life.

St. John of the Cross (1542–1591), was a Spanish Carmelite reformer, mystical writer, and doctor of the Church.

Pope John Paul II (1920–2005), reigned as pope for almost twenty-seven years and played a key role in the fall of communism. He is one of the most beloved popes of the modern era and is called "Pope John Paul the Great."

St. Jeanne Jugan (1792–1879), the foundress and first Little Sister of the Poor, devoted her life to the care of the elderly poor. On October 11, 2009, she was canonized by Pope Benedict XVI.

St. Julian of Norwich (1342–1423), a hermit and one of the greatest English mystics, wrote about God's merciful love and compassion.

Msgr. Ronald Knox (1888–1957), was an Anglican convert to Catholicism and the Catholic chaplain at Oxford. He translated the Bible and wrote dozens of books explaining the Catholic faith with clarity, wisdom, and wit.

St. Maximilian Kolbe (1894–1941), was a Polish Franciscan priest and founder of the Knights of Mary Immaculate. His martyrdom in Auschwitz was said to be "like a powerful shaft of light in the darkness of the camp."

St. Faustina Kowalska (1905–1938), was a Polish nun and mystic who, after receiving visions of Jesus, introduced the popular devotion to Divine Mercy.

Peter Kreeft, PH.D. (1939—), a convert to Catholicism, is a professor of philosophy at Boston College and a well-known author and speaker.

Brother Lawrence (1614–1691), was a member of the Discalced Carmelite monastery in Paris. He was known for his profound peace and wisdom, which became the basis for the book *The Practice of the Presence of God*.

St. Paul Le-Bao-Tinh (d. 1857), was a Vietnamese priest who was martyred by the emperor for his refusal to renounce his Catholic faith.

Servant of God Elisabeth Leseur (1866–1914), lived a life of simplicity amid the swirl of Parisian society. She used her serious illness and her husband's constant efforts to destroy her faith as means to grow in love for him and for God.

Clive Staples Lewis (1898–1963), commonly referred to as C.S. Lewis, was an Irish-born British novelist, academic, theologian, and Christian apologist. He is also known for his fiction, especially *The Screwtape Letters* and *The Chronicles of Narnia*.

St. Alphonsus Liguori (1696–1787), was a bishop and founder of the Congregation of the Most Holy Redeemer.

George MacDonald (1824–1905), was one of the most respected authors of his generation in nineteenth-century Scotland. His writings, more than fifty books, had a significant impact on the conversion of C.S. Lewis.

Msgr. Peter Magee (1958—), is a former member of the diplomatic service of the Vatican, a university professor, and the author of several articles on spiritual, theological, and canonical topics.

Ralph Martin is the president of Renewal Ministries, an organization devoted to Catholic renewal and evangelization, and the host of the weekly television program *The Choices We Face*. He is the author of the best-selling book *The Fulfillment of All Desire* and the director of graduate programs in the New Evangelization at Sacred Heart Seminary in Detroit, Michigan.

St. Thomas More (1478–1535), a lawyer, scholar, author, husband, father, and lord chancellor of England, was martyred for his principled faith. He is known for his courage and fortitude in the face of death.

Malcolm Muggeridge (1903–1990), was a British journalist, social critic, and author. An avowed atheist, he moved gradually toward Roman Catholicism and embraced the faith at age seventy-nine.

Fr. Aidan Mullaney, T.O.R., (1925—), is a Franciscan friar, a poet, and a writer.

Bl. Cardinal John Henry Newman (1801–1890), was a prolific English author who converted from Anglicanism to Catholicism and became an Oratorian priest and cardinal.

Fr. Henri Nouwen (1932–1996), was a Dutch-born Catholic priest and writer who taught at influential universities for almost two decades before joining Daybreak L'Arche community in Canada, where he lived and worked with the mentally challenged until his death.

Flannery O'Connor (1925–1964), was a southern American whose writing often reflected her Catholic faith and frequently examined questions of morals and ethics.

St. Patrick of Ireland (circa 389–circa 461), British or perhaps Gallic, was a bishop and missionary known as "The Apostle of the Irish."

St. Paul of the Cross (1694–1775), was an Italian monk, a preacher, and the founder and first superior general of the Passionists.

Pope Paul VI (1897–1978), reigned as pope from 1963 to 1978. He presided over the final sessions of the Second Vatican Council, appointed commissions to carry out its reforms, and promoted ecumenism.

St. Padre Pio of Pietrelcina (1887–1968), was a Capuchin priest and mystic who bore the wounds of Christ on his body.

Pope St. Pius X (1835–1914), was a catalyst of the liturgical renewal who promoted frequent Communion.

Fr. Michael Scanlan, T.O.R., (1931—), is the former dean and current chancellor of Franciscan University of Steubenville and the author of many books on practical wisdom for the Christian life.

Mother Basilea Schlink (1904–2001), founded the Evangelical Sisterhood of Mary in post-war Germany. She wrote prolifically about how to walk the pathway of the cross with joy.

Cardinal Christoph Schönborn (1945—), the archbishop of Vienna, Austria, is a highly regarded author and coeditor of the *Catechism of the Catholic Church*.

St. Elizabeth Ann Seton (1774–1821), the first native-born citizen of the United States to be canonized by the Roman Catholic Church, was a wife and mother and the foundress of the Sisters of Charity. She is popularly considered a patron saint of Catholic schools.

The Most Reverend Fulton J. Sheen (1895–1979), was an American bishop and author known for his preaching and especially for his work on television and radio.

Alexander Solzhenitsyn (1918–2008), was a Russian novelist and historian whose writings exposed the Soviet Union's forced labor camp system. He was awarded the Nobel Prize in Literature in 1970, was exiled from the Soviet Union in 1974, and returned to Russia in 1994.

St. Teresa Benedicta of the Cross (Edith Stein) (1891–1942), was a brilliant professor of philosophy who converted from Judaism and eventually joined the Carmelites. She and her sister Rose died at the hands of the Nazis at Auschwitz.

St. Teresa of Avila (1515–1582), also known as Teresa of Jesus, was a Spanish mystic, a great reformer of the Carmelite order, and a doctor of the Church.

Bl. Teresa of Calcutta (1910–1997), was an Albanian Catholic nun with Indian citizenship who founded the Missionaries of Charity in Calcutta in 1950 and won the Nobel Peace Prize in 1979.

St. Thérèse of the Child Jesus (1873–1897), also known as Thérèse of Lisieux, was a French Carmelite nun, mystic, and doctor of the Church. One of the most popular saints of the twentieth century, she was canonized less than thirty years after her death at the age of twenty-four and is best known for her "Little Way" to holiness.

J.R.R. Tolkien (1892–1973), was an English writer, poet, philologist, and university professor, best known as the author of the classic high fantasy works *The Hobbit* and *The Lord of the Rings*.

Fr. Simon Tugwell, O.P., is a British Dominican priest and the author of several books on theology and spirituality.

Jean Vanier (1928—), is a Swiss Catholic philosopher and author and the founder of L'Arche, an international organization that creates communities where people with developmental disabilities and those who assist them live and work together.

Cardinal Francis Xavier Nguyen Van Thuan (1928–2002), a leader in renewal and evangelization in Asia, was imprisoned in communist Vietnam for more than thirteen years, nine of which were spent in solitary confinement, and eventually exiled from his homeland.

Dom Hubert van Zeller (1905–1984), a Benedictine monk in England, was a sculptor and writer of over fifty books on the spiritual life.

St. Théophane Vénard (1829–1861), entered the Foreign Missions of Paris and was ordained and sent to Vietnam two years later. He taught in a seminary until his arrest and brutal martyrdom.

Dietrich von Hildebrand (1889–1977), a convert to Catholicism, was a German philosopher, theologian, and author.

Margery Williams (1881–1944), was an English-American author, primarily of popular children's books. She achieved lasting fame with the 1922 publication of the classic *The Velveteen Rabbit*.

The

Sources

1. Pope Benedict XVI, *Spe Salvi: Saved in Hope*, no. 27 (Ijamsville, Md.: Word Among Us, 2007), p. 43.

2. Henri Nouwen, *Jesus, A Gospel*, Michael O'Laughlin, ed. (New York: Orbis, 2001), p. 104.

3. John Henry Newman, adapted from *Selected Sermons, Prayers, and Devotions*, John F. Thornton and Susan B. Varenne, eds. (New York: Vintage, 1999), p. 205.

4. Francis de Sales, quoted in Francis W. Johnston, ed., *The Voice of the Saints* (Rockford, Ill.: Tan, 1965), p. 132.

5. Julian of Norwich, *Revelations of Divine Love*, Clifton Wolters, trans. (London: Penguin, 1986), pp. 184–185.

6. George MacDonald, "Obedience," in Regis Martin, ed., *Images of Grace: Thirty-three Christian Poems* (Steubenville, Ohio: Franciscan University Press, 1995), pp. 26–27.

7. Paul Le-Bao-Tinh, quoted in Benedict XVI, *Saved in Hope*, pp. 56–57.

8. Benedict Groeschel, *Arise From Darkness: When Life Doesn't Make Sense* (San Francisco: Ignatius, 1995), p. 132.

9. Jean-Pierre de Caussade, *Abandonment to Divine Providence* (New York: Image, 1975), pp. 83–84.

10. Anselm, *Proslogion*, quoted in John Bartunek, *The Better Part: A Christ-Centered Resource for Personal Prayer* (Hamden, Conn.: Circle, 2007), p. 112.

11. Antony the Great, quoted in Paul Thigpen, *A Dictionary of Quotes From the Saints* (Ann Arbor, Mich.: Charis, 2001), p. 230.

12. John Henry Newman, adapted from *Prayers, Verses, and Devotions* (San Francisco: Ignatius, 2000), p. 339.

13. Brother Lawrence, adapted from *The Practice of the Presence of God* (Old Tappan, N.J.: Spire, 1974), pp. 55, 57.

14. Edith Stein, "Weihnachtsgeheimnis," in *Wege zur inneren Stille,* collected articles, W. Herbstrith, ed. (Frankfurt: Kaffke Verlage, 1978), p. 14, quoted in Waltraud Herbstrith, *Edith Stein: A Biography*, Bernard Bonowitz, trans. (San Francisco: Ignatius, 1992), p. 154.

15. Pope John Paul II, *Lessons for Living* (Chicago: Loyola, 2004), p. 38.

16. J.R.R. Tolkien, *The Lord of the Rings*, pt. 3, *The Return of the King* (New York: Ballantine, 1994), p. 194.

17. Julian of Norwich, *Revelations*, p. 87.

18. Teresa of Avila, quoted in Johnston, p. 121.

19. Thomas à Kempis, *The Imitation of Christ* (Garden City, N.Y.: Image, 1955), p. 94.

20. Nouwen, *Jesus, A Gospel*, p. 57.

21. Pope John Paul II, Homily, Seventeenth World Youth Day, Solemn Mass, Toronto, July 28, 2002, www.vatican.va.

22. Bernard of Clairvaux, quoted in Ralph Martin, *The Fulfillment of All Desire: A Guidebook for the Journey to God Based on the Wisdom of the Saints* (Steubenville, Ohio: Emmaus Road, 2006), pp. 163–164.

23. Words of Jesus to Faustina Kowalska, quoted in Bartunek, p. 251.

24. Michael Scanlan with Jim Manney, *The Truth About Trouble: How Hard Times Can Draw You Closer to God* (Cincinnati: Servant, 2005), pp. 77–78.

25. Padre Pio, quoted in Charles Mortimer Carty, *Padre Pio: The Stigmatist* (Rockford, Ill.: Tan, 2009), p. 247.

26. Francis de Sales, quoted in Thigpen, *A Dictionary of Quotes from the Saints*, p. 236.

27. De Caussade, *Abandonment to Divine Providence*, p. 82.

28. Adapted from Thomas à Kempis, *The Imitation of Christ*, pp. 198–199.

29. Nouwen, *Jesus, A Gospel*, pp. 91–92.

30. Paul of the Cross, quoted in Thigpen, *A Dictionary of Quotes from the Saints*, p. 224.

31. Dietrich von Hildebrand, *Confidence in God* (Manchester, N.H.: Sophia Institute, 1997), pp. 62–63.

32. Pope Benedict XVI, *Spe Salvi*, no. 32, pp. 49–50.

33. Pope John Paul II, *Lessons for Living*, p. 95.

34. Henri J.M. Nouwen, *A Cry for Mercy: Prayers from the Genesee* (Garden City, N.Y.: Doubleday, 1981), pp. 28, 29.

35. Claude de la Colombière, in Jean Baptiste Saint-Jure and Claude de la Colombière, *Trustful Surrender to Divine Providence*, Paul Garvin, trans. (Rockford, Ill.: Tan, 1983), p. 107.

36. Malcolm Muggeridge, quoted in Kurt Bruner and Jim Ware, *Finding God in the Lord of the Rings* (Wheaton, Ill.: Tyndale, 2006), pp. 75–76.

37. Bernard of Clairvaux, quoted in Bartunek, p. 164.

38. Thomas Aquinas, quoted in Bartunek, p. 419.

39. Padre Pio, quoted in Carty, p. 247.

40. Josemaría Escrivá, *The Way*, no. 722 (London: Scepter, 1985), p. 250.

41. Augustine, quoted in Bartunek, p. 192.

42. Dom Hubert van Zeller, *Suffering in Other Words: A Presentation for Beginners* (Springfield, Ill.: Templegate, 1964), p. 82.

43. Peter Kreeft, *Making Sense Out of Suffering* (Ann Arbor, Mich.: Servant, 1986), pp. 144–145.

44. Cyprian, quoted in Bartunek, p. 89.

45. Simon Tugwell, quoted in *Magnificat*, vol. 10, no. 13 (February 2009), p. 106.

46. Teresa of Ávila, quoted in Bartunek, p. 633.

47. Francois de Salignac de La Mothe Fénelon, *Let Go* (New Kensington, Pa.: Whitaker House, 1973), pp. 33–34.

48. Pope Gregory the Great, quoted in Bartunek, p. 675.

49. De Caussade, *Abandonment to Divine Providence*, p. 95.

50. Ralph Martin, *Renewal Ministries Newsletter*, January 2008, p. 3.

51. John of the Cross, *The Dark Night*, 11, 9, 1, quoted in Francis Kelly Nemeck and Marie Theresa Coombs, *O Blessed Night: Recovering from Addiction, Codependency and Attachment based on the insights of St. John of the Cross and Pierre Teilhard de Chardin* (Staten Island, N.Y.: Alba House, 1991), p. 86.

52. Cardinal John Henry Newman, "The Second Spring," sermon quoted in Charles Frederick Harrold, ed., *A Newman Treasury* (London: Longmans Green, 1943), p. 221.

53. William J. Bennett, *The Moral Compass: Stories for a Life's Journey* (New York: Simon & Schuster, 1995), pp. 245, 246.

54. Teresa of Avila, adapted from Christopher Rengers, ed., *The 33 Doctors of the Church* (Rockford, Ill.: Tan, 2000), p. 450.

55. Pope Benedict XVI, *Saved in Hope*, no. 30, p. 47.

56. Thérèse of the Child Jesus, quoted in A.A. Noser, *Joy in Suffering: According to St. Thérèse of the Child Jesus* (Rockford, Ill.: Tan, 2009), pp. 69–70.

57. Théophane Vénard, adapted from Johnston, p. 127.

58. Cardinal Basil Hume, adapted from *To Be a Pilgrim: A Spiritual Notebook* (Australia: St. Paul, 2009), p. 72–73.

59. John of the Cross, quoted in Nemeck and Coombs, p. 87.

60. Elisabeth Leseur, quoted in Cynthia Cavnar, *The Saints' Guide to Help When Life Hurts* (Ann Arbor, Mich.: Servant, 2001), p. 70.

61. John Paul II, *Lessons for Living*, p. 62.

62. John Chrysostom, quoted in Bartunek, p. 376.

63. Pope Paul VI, *Pensiero alla Morte* [Thoughts on Death], *L'Osservatore Romano*, August 5, 1979, p. 5, quoted in Francis Xavier Nguyen Van Thuan, *Testimony of Hope: The Spiritual Exercises of John Paul II* (Chicago: Pauline, 2000), p. 57.

64. Aidan Mullaney, "On the Night of Hugo," in Regis Martin, pp. 44–45.

65. Thomas More, quoted in Ronda De Sola Chervin, ed., *Quotable Saints* (Ann Arbor, Mich.: Servant, 2003), p. 101.

66. Augustine, quoted in Bartunek, p. 176.

67. Peter Magee, adapted from *God's Mercy Revealed: Healing for a Broken World* (Cincinnati: Servant, 2005), p. 112.

68. Van Thuan, p. 93.

69. Henri Nouwen, *Can You Drink the Cup?* (Notre Dame, Ind.: Ave Maria, 1997), pp. 50–51.

70. M. Basilea Schlink, adapted from *Strong in the Time of Testing* (Darmstadt, Germany: Evangelical Sisterhood of Mary, 1993), p. 15.

71. Francois de Salignac de La Mothe Fénelon, *The Seeking Heart*, vol. 4, *Library of Spiritual Classics* (Jacksonville, Fla.: SeedSowers, 1992), p. 73.

72. Jean-Pierre de Caussade, *The Joy of Full Surrender*, Hal M. Helms, ed. (Brewster, Mass.: Paraclete, 1986), p. 87.

73. Brother Lawrence, *The Practice of the Presence of God,* quoted in Benedict Groeschel and Bert Ghezzi, *Everyday Encounters With God: What Our Experiences Teach Us About the Divine* (Ijamsville, Md.: Word Among Us, 2008), p. 141.

74. Margery Williams, *The Velveteen Rabbit: Or How Toys Become Real* (New York: Doubleday, 1958), pp. 5–6.

75. Elisabeth Leseur, *A Wife's Story*, quoted in Cavnar, p. 93.

76. Donald De Marco, *The Heart of Virtue: Lessons from Life and Literature Illustrating the Beauty and Value of Moral Character* (San Francisco: Ignatius, 1996), pp. 110, 111–112.

77. Alphonsus Liguori, quoted in Johnston, pp. 118–119.

78. Á Kempis, p. 46.
79. John Chrysostom, quoted in Chervin, pp. 99–100.
80. Faustina Kowalska, quoted in Van Thuan, p. 58.
81. Fénelon, *Let Go*, p. 80.
82. Braulio of Saragossa, quoted in LaVonne Neff, ed., *Breakfast With the Saints: Daily Readings from Great Christians* (Ann Arbor, Mich.: Servant, 1996), p. 25.
83. Magee, p. 128.
84. Maximilian Kolbe, quoted in Ferdinand Holböck, *New Saints and Blesseds of the Catholic Church*, Michael J. Miller, trans. (Fort Collins, Colo.: Ignatius, 2003), vol. 1, p. 200.
85. Elizabeth Ann Seton, adapted from *A Daily Thought From the Writings of Mother Seton,* Joseph B. Code, ed. (Emmitsburg, Md.: Sisters of Charity of St. Vincent de Paul, 1929), no. 12.
86. John of Karpathos, quoted in Neff, p. 85.
87. Pope John Paul II, Address at Lourdes, France, May 22, 1979, quoted in Margaret R. Bunson, ed., *John Paul II's Book of Mary* (Huntington, Ind.: Our Sunday Visitor, 2005), pp. 137–138.
88. Isidore of Seville, quoted in Johnston, pp. 125–126.
89. Catherine de Hueck Doherty, *Dearly Beloved: Letters to the Children of My Spirit, Volume Three, 1974–1983* (Combermere, Ontario: Madonna House, 1990), pp. 85, 86.
90. Jerome, quoted in Johnston, p. 118.
91. Van Thuan, p. 205.
92. Bernard of Clairvaux, quoted in Ralph Martin, *Fulfillment of All Desire*, p. 442.
93. Pius X, quoted in Johnston, p. 130.
94. Thomas Dubay, *Saints: A Closer Look* (Cincinnati: Servant, 2007), p. 134.
95. Patrick, quoted in Bartunek, p. 834.
96. Cardinal John Henry Newman, "The Pillar of the Cloud," in Regis Martin, pp. 17–18.
97. Fénelon, *The Seeking Heart*, p. 14.
98. Julian of Norwich, quoted in Gloria Durka, *Praying with Julian of Norwich* (Winona, Minn.: St. Mary's, 1995), p. 100.
99. Fulton J. Sheen, *Way to Happiness* (Garden City, N.Y.: Garden City, 1954), pp. 191–192.
100. Groeschel, *Everyday Encounters with God*, p. 123.

101. Jean Vanier, *Be Not Afraid* (Toronto: Griffin, 1975), p. 145.

102. Terence J. Cooke, quoted in Paul Thigpen, *Last Words: Final Thoughts of Catholic Saints & Sinners* (Cincinnati: Servant, 2006), p. 14.

103. Immaculée Ilibagiza, *Left to Tell: Discovering God Amidst the Rwandan Holocaust* (Carlsbad, Calif.: Hay House, 2006), pp. 130–131.

104. C.S. Lewis, *The Business of Heaven: Daily Readings From C.S. Lewis*, Walter Hooper, ed. (New York: Harcourt Brace, 1984), p. 244.

105. Teresa of Calcutta, adapted from *The Joy in Loving: A Guide to Daily Living with Mother Teresa* (New York: Viking, 1996), p. 215.

106. Jeanne Jugan, quoted in Paul Milcent, *Jeanne Jugan: Humble, So As to Love More*, Alan Neame, trans. (London: Darton, Longman & Todd, 1981), p. 202.

107. John Chrysostom, quoted in Anne Field, *From Darkness to Light* (Ann Arbor, Mich.: Servant, 1978), pp. 33–34.

108. Cardinal Joseph Ratzinger, *Milestones: Memoirs 1927–1977*, Erasmo Leiva-Merikakis, trans. (San Francisco: Ignatius, 1998), p. 131.

109. Augustine, adapted from Field, p. 92.

110. Ronald A. Knox, *The Window in the Wall: Reflections on the Holy Eucharist* (New York: Sheed & Ward, 1956), pp. 112–113.

111. Dorothy Day, *House of Hospitality*, quoted in Woodeene Koenig-Bricker, *Meet Dorothy Day: Champion of the Poor* (Ann Arbor, Mich.: Charis, 2002), p. 132.

112. The Desert Fathers, adapted from Helen Waddell, *The Desert Fathers* (New York: Vintage, 1998), p. 159.

113. Frances Xavier Cabrini, quoted in Bert Ghezzi, *The Heart of a Saint: Ten Ways to Grow Closer to God* (Ijamsville, Md.: Word Among Us, 2007), p. 140.

114. Flannery O'Connor, *Mystery and Manners*, Sally and Robert Fitzgerald, eds. (New York: Farrar, Straus & Giroux, 1969), p. 113.

115. Caryll Houselander, *The Way of the Cross* (Liguori, Mo.: Liguori, 2002), p. 28.

116. Aleksandr Solzhenitsyn, quoted in Joseph Pearce, *Solzhenitsyn: A Soul in Exile* (Grand Rapids: Baker, 1999), p. 308.

117. Gerard Manley Hopkins, *Mortal Beauty, God's Grace: Major Poems and Spiritual Writings of Gerard Manley Hopkins*, John F. Thornton and Susan B. Varenne, eds. (New York: Vintage, 2003), pp. 145–146.

118. Antiochus, quoted in Frederick William Faber, *All for Jesus: The Easy Ways of Divine Love* (Manchester, N.H.: Sophia Institute, 2000), p. 183.

119. Cardinal Christoph Schönborn, adapted from *My Jesus: Encountering Jesus in the Gospel* (San Francisco: Ignatius, 2005), p. 90.

120. Raniero Cantalamessa, quoted in Ann Shields, *Hope in the Midst of Suffering* (Ann Arbor, Mich.: Renewal Ministries, 2003), pp. 21–22.

ABOUT THE AUTHOR

Debra Herbeck works extensively in youth and women's ministries and is the producer for the weekly Catholic television program *The Choices We Face.* She is the newsletter editor for Renewal Ministries and coauthor, with her husband, Peter, of *When the Spirit Speaks: Touched by God's Word* (Servant). The Herbecks live in Ann Arbor, Michigan, and are the parents of four children.